THE TRUTH IN RENTED ROOMS

THE **TRUTH** IN RENTED ROOMS

for Dr Ying Zhang Chen

Best wishes,

— Koon Woon

KOON WOON

FOREWORD BY RUSSELL LEONG

Kaya 1998

Portions of this book have previously appeared in
Asian Pacific American Journal, Bellowing Ark, Black Spring Review, Bumbershoot Anthology, HELLP!, Hell's Kitchen, Irresistible Impulse, Lucid Moon, Only Connect, Pididdle, Real Change, and *Seattle Review.*

Published by Kaya
132 West 22nd Street, 4th Floor
New York, NY 10011
(212) 352-9220 www.kaya.com

Book design by Erin Shigaki

Manufactured in the United States of America

Distributed by D.A.P./Distributed Art Publishers
155 Avenue of the Americas, 2nd Floor
New York, NY 10013
(800) 338-BOOK www.artbook.com

ISBN 1-885030-25-8
Library of Congress Catalog Card Number: 98-66816

Many thanks to Juliana Koo, Sunyoung Lee, Sesshu Foster, Robert Kuwada, and Russell Leong for creating a literary community and inviting me in. I am also indebted to the encouragements of my teachers Carolyn Maddux, Allen Hikida, and the late Nelson Bentley.

And with warm personal regards, this book is dedicated to Allen and Charlotte Henkins, Betty Priebe, my uncle Li Gar Sum, and my brothers and sisters.

— Koon Woon

CONTENTS

THE MORRISON (1993–1996)

INTERNATIONAL TERRACE (1996–1998)

FOREWORD

"what is 'the truth in rented rooms'?" asks a reader

In the poetry of Koon Woon, what is "the truth in rented rooms"? Does truth "live in a boat of paper" to borrow lines from one of his own poems? Or must we delve into the "psychoanalysis of a room," or even sweep up "three drops of blood on the butcher's sawdust floor"? Meanwhile, "the rest of the furniture squats in the cold and dark, complains of being a lone man's furnishings, and plots a revolt." Each word and wall of Koon Woon's room asks a question, but I am looking for an answer.

At first, I think the truth lies in Koon Woon's perfect ability to capture places — whether it is a tenement building in Seattle, the kitchen of his father's Chinese American restaurant, a palace in some Chinese emperor's real estate holdings, the confines of a psychiatric halfway house, or the succession of spartan single rooms that the poet has inhabited most of his life. But as I read on, his rooms expand in my mind, becoming windows that reveal whole generations of women and men in transit in their lives, magnified under the calming light of Koon Woon's compassion. Or, perhaps the room is a refuge, where the writer can comfort himself "with tea and the religiosity of sesame crackers."

Well, yes, and no. The room in the poem "The Slowness of Days" is a paean to lovemaking and the journey "from the center of love to the extremities of fingertips and toes." Then I hear Koon Woon differently — pacing through the "underheated, intrepid rooms" in "I've Heard the Chan Bells of the Monastery." So I wander from room to unadorned room in my search for some poetic truth in a faithless age.

A door suddenly opens. Koon Woon, turning his face to the window, begins to read "Apple Moment": "I was a snail, I hauled my house/Equidistant from you, A flower on an apple bough...." I realize I have gotten waylaid by the particulars of place, by the beauty of his lyrics, and by my own ethnocentricism, being a person who also grew up and inhabited rented rooms in a Chinatown barrio after the Second World War. Waylaid — for I realize in Koon Woon's moment of "apple" that the truth does not lie literally within four Chinatown walls lit by a single light bulb, if at all. That an apple is an apple as much as it is also a room. That the room is merely a permeable lens through which Koon Woon observes and writes the world. That the room, in all its manifestations and moments, is a space that he carries within him wherever he travels.

It was not until I began to study the poetry of Koon Woon that my preconceptions, like old walls, tumbled down, and my eyelids, like closed curtains fluttered open: suddenly, the faces and voices of ordinary people became vivid and audible to me. Such epiphany rarely occurs in poetry, and rarer still in rented rooms. Why? I asked Sesshu Foster, the Los Angeles poet and teacher who selected the poetry included in this volume. Why? I asked Alan Chong Lau, the Seattle artist who first introduced Koon Woon's work to me in 1990. They urged me to trust my truest feelings, and they were right.

Perhaps Koon Woon's acute description of his father would clue me:

How my father, his back curving more each year
From the weight of the morning air,
The ever-increasing weight of wife and eight children,
All permissible dreams and sorrows clinging on like grapes,
That in the unofficial histories of his veins,
Bombs dropped near his village, metal and body parts flew;
The naked bulb here was the same naked bulb on Angel Island,
detained there because he was an immigrant, a Chinese immigrant…

Under the harsh light of detention in a new land, Koon Woon's poems emerge as part of the "unofficial history" of Asian American (read American) literature that is barely recognized by publishers, middle-brow Asian American academic types, or by poetry foundations and literati elites. Like the Angel Island poems carved on the walls of detention barracks by early Asian immigrants, like inner-city graffiti sprayed or chiseled on walls and buildings, like posters for democracy pasted on walls in Tiananmen Square, Koon Woon's poems possess a moral intention that is part of the consciousness of struggling peoples everywhere. If his odes are unofficial, their calibrations and calculations on the plaster or drywall of rented rooms leave marks as vital as breathing. These poems, taken as a whole, form the backbone and reality of the marginalized in America — of immigrants and refugees, workers and women, the poor, renters, halfway house recoverees — those whose voices and expression have traditionally not been sought or heard, recognized or taught, canonized or collected by others.

In the poet's own words, his work is shaped by "the richly needed human bondage on both of our parts." His poems are thus "necessary gestures" that arise out of work and compassion for a community larger than himself; they resonate with the social consciousness and lyric impulse of the German poet, Bertolt Brecht. Yet, ultimately, his lyrics are shaped by his hands and eyes alone, within his rented room, with his books of T. S. Eliot, Li Po, Jean Follain, César Vallejo, and others stacked neatly in a corner.

As Koon Woon looks out the window at a misty Seattle sky, recalling the fateful day he arrived in America at the age of eleven, he thinks of his life in terms of the interior rooms he creates, for:

In my room the world is true
Simply because I say it is true

...

Parallel rooms that connect like the sections
Of a dragon, one black and one golden,
Interwoven and locked in mortal combat....

Koon Woon crosses from room to room: we hear the mortal footsteps of his sleeplessness in his passages. One room is redolent of Canton; another of Seattle. One room holds the father, the other clasps the son. One room contains the meter of music; another sustains the measure of the mathematics he loves. One person drinks tea at home; another, homeless, drinks cold coffee from a paper cup in Pioneer Square, Seattle. Here, Koon Woon finds love in one room and nurtures solitude in the same place, buddhistically, without discrimination or recrimination.

As for us — impoverished readers of poetry — we must be grateful for the rented room that Koon Woon has kindly provided us. Temporary boarders, we discover, with astonishment, humility, and pleasure, that the rooms expand through his words to "fill all the spaces of the universe not already occupied by atoms...."

Russell Leong
Editor, *Amerasia Journal*
University of California, Los Angeles

7th AVENUE SOUTH

1985 – 1992

The Question I want to ask

A command sets a thousand horses galloping
while a question merely drops a frog into a pond.
Elsewhere the required question is not the same.
Elsewhere they ask for rain, for harvests, and for newborns
to pick up the heavy plows.
Elsewhere there are infants to pick up, messages to scurry.
One nation is on fire, another in revolt, still a third one quakes.

I peer out at the pond. I am the dwarf of Socrates
looking at humanity, the midget of Isaac Newton looking
at the invisible gravity.
The frog sits on a single lotus leaf, its eyes pinhole cameras
to record its domain,
from an ill-defined mosquito to a very deliberate water snake.

It has been ten years since the frog leaped from my mouth.
At water's edge, the water lilies have transformed
from buds to jungle foliage, and every cell in my body
has been washed and replaced.
Grassy fields have turned golden, then brown.

I ask the wind if it would listen.
Elsewhere the wind sweeps a fire across a prairie.
The pond, now smooth as a bald man's head,
swallows my question but gives no answer.
But I am no longer disappointed that it is so, and
the thousand horses that went galloping
return now of their own accord.

The Memory of hands

In memory of my grandmother

I. In Water Buffalo Time

Honey-auntie collects bees in her palm:
When she says Go! they fly off to sue the flowers.
And when she says Come Back! they roll their honey-
bellies in her hand.

Uncles arc in rice paddies, itching where leeches suck
their legs.

I sprinkle Grandmother's garden of bokchoy, cabbages,
and wintermelons heavy like little buddhas.

Grandmother gets wood and gossip from Firewood-auntie,
and pays her a few bronze coins to light incense.
Both women's husbands died three decades ago,
leaving them the void of Confucian hands.

At dusk my grandmother trots out in her bound feet to retrieve
the drying vegetables hung on a bamboo pole like the character
jen (people).

The sun drops behind the last rice paddy
as the water buffalo sinks in the village pond,
dropping dung for black shrimps.
And at last Grandmother draws the mosquito net
in the lychee-pit night.

II. Sampan

A journey in yellow water. I am sick
and Grandmother tells me to think of not moving.
Think of a place far away like Gimshan, she says.
Do not move against the river and you will be still.
Don't resist the womb's muscles to deliver you.
Your head was so big we used forceps,
and now you are a cavern
for three bowls of rice and pigs' feet stewed in rice vinegar!

Grandmother is not moving although the boat moves.
She tells me to think of lemon.

The boatman, pushing the river bottom with his long bamboo pole,
carries all the land he cares for in his sampan.
As I become better, I awe at his calves.

The river I know must have fish.
The fish must look up at the shadow that moves.
The fish move in a moving river,
But I am still because Grandmother is still.

We are leaving the village for Canton.
The chrysanthemums are in bloom just now,
And Gimshan is where I must soon go.

III. The World's Longest Alley

For a snip of cloth Grandmother took my hand
and led me through bicycle-laden streets,
past shoppers by fours, past wine and vinegar stores.
Buses overtook us.
And finally, walking as far as three rolls
of cloth would unroll,
we arrived at the entrance of the world's longest alley,
where vendors on both sides set up
painted fans, brilliantly glazed pottery,
and cloth of every color
as they haggled with shoppers,
squeezing the alley like a tourniquet on a blood vessel.

Grandmother: "The five colors blind the eye!"
But she doesn't heed Lao Tsu and slides her fingers
on the rolls of exquisite cloth.
We hear it is exported.

But there are no candy vendors, though there's a man
who has taught his monkey to beg with a tipped hat.

The alley is long as a conversation with a river.
In the colorful blur, she assents to an ice-cream bar.
I am then happy for coming along,
for the first time I see
Grandmother as a maiden of sixteen,
her young eyes dazzled by the dowry of cloth.

IV. The Memory of Hands

If you fold a piece of paper once, then unfold it,
it will tend toward the folded position. That's because
the paper has "memory."

The memory of hands, of ancient vine.
My monsoon eyes, my face, tilled by fingers.
A chicken plucked gently naked.
Hands, unable to sign a legal signature,
close the fan,
and draw the mosquito net.

At the Hong Kong International Airport, I took a mental
photograph of my grandmother. A young girl wrings free of
her mother's hand and runs along, laughing.

Her index finger wrote a whorl on my back to designate an ox.
My hands, curved upward to suggest valleys of space,
would squeeze water,
would cling to ancient vine,
would throw   a marble across the river.

The loudspeaker announces, announces last call, last call.
Third-aunt says hurry, hurry, or you will miss your future.

The past folds up like an origami bird,
will not dissolve like candy.
Grapes cling to the vine, hands weave bamboo baskets,
hands supplicate and light incense,
Buddha holds her in his palm.
I fold paper for hands of ancient vine,
hands that couldn't come along.
And hands will open gates if I should return.

Gimshan is Cantonese for America, literally Golden Mountain.

Windows after a rain

My window-framed face peers out,
The matrix of graded streets, stratified
Urban achievements. In the alley,
Puddles connect like children holding hands.

While rain snared windows, I sat reading
A Tale of Two Cities. I was a lost thought
Among the closet's forgotten thoughts; now

The sunlight gushes in and conquers me,
A solar cell, a reluctant melon, a crow perched
On the intelligentsia of a telephone pole.

Sparrows clutch phone wires to frisk out insincere notes of lovers;
Pigeons reclaim city squares;
I take the thermometer out of my mouth;

It had garbled my speech while eloquent voices
Fought for column inches. This light,
Without which existence is not detectable, is

A universal Einstein loved so well, it conquers
The dark corners of my room as I comfort myself
With tea and the religiosity of sesame crackers.

Raw and easy

1.
Nightly, there is no bottom.
I wrap myself in my quilt.
With my scarred past rotten,
I abuse myself to the hilt.

My eyes report to the skull
what the dark corners bring.
My ears deliver gossip to
lead me to an early drink.

Thoughts reduce to pins;
these I insert into my bones.
Passions magnify into rivers,
two rivers against the sea.

Nightly, like blades of scissors,
my life and death meet to divide;
they argue over me like hungry
merchants, to get the lowest price.

2.
Ships float out with the night's remnants.
I seize the orange in the sky.
I peel the minutes, anxious,
waiting for the roll of the die.

With my nakedness redeemed,
I examine all my veins.
Blood surges within the body,
dividing me into roads and lanes.

In circles, my thoughts are tongue-tied;
I pray and I utter just one sound.
Ah, I have not left land yet,
my anchor is still on the ground.

3.
With my eyes half-open, I
lie embedded; my loins aroused
by the pristine current, I
will be worn smooth, like

a piece of jade dangling
from the ear of an exquisite
woman, hearing everything
she hears.

I am often tempted to abandon
my house and mantlepiece,
to travel raw and easy, to connect
my nerve with every eel and owl.

I am easy and lazy, my eyes
lenses in the forest, with
every fern calling my name,
I shall say I know; I know

sand and water will cut any stone.
Time, that is, is all there is.
If I die, I'll die before my bones.
This is what I know and just this.

The water keeps ebbing fast,
ebbing past, it contains many tunes.
The time I listened last,
it contained even my tune.

Cold stones

Would copper coins and amulets
from the Sung Dynasty
dispel these ghosts of regret?
We sat, face to face,
at a tea-house in Tien-An.

I call upon your name,
the old man from Nan-On.
Perhaps one should say:
"This tea comes from the high hills of…"
Or perhaps,
"This tea cup is an old relic…"

We reach into our pockets to find words
but only possess
cold stones.
The cups are emptied
and emptied again,
with the rapidity of
a school boy rattling off
the names of the dynasties.

We are old men, forever parting,
never joining.
This is the schism:
not by waters and not by years,
but by glances that implore
and by words that fail us.
When we reach into our pockets
for something to give —
cold stones.

Soul to soul, we had never met.
Our little wars had drawn us together.
Now there is peace over the hills.
Now peasants are rebuilding huts.
Can we now repair ourselves?
Or must we, like condemned men,
carry cold stones in our pockets?

Goldfish

The goldfish in my bowl
turns into a carp each night.
Swimming in circles in the day,
regal, admired by emperors,
but each night, while I sleep,
it turns into silver, a dagger
cold and sharp, couched at one spot,
enough to frighten cats.

The rest of the furniture
squats in the cold and dark,
complains of being a lone man's
furnishings, and plots a revolt.
I can hear myself snore, but not
their infidelity. Sometimes I wake
with a start, silently they move back
into their places.

I have been unpopular with myself,
pacing in my small, square room,
but my uncle said, "Even in a palace,
you can but sleep in one room."
With this I become humble as a simple
preacher, saying, "I have no powers;
they emanate from God."
With this I sleep soundly,

Fish or no fish, dagger or no dagger.
When I wake, my fish is gold,
it pleases me with a trail of bubbles.
My furniture has been loyal all night,
waiting to provide me comfort.
There was no conspiracy against a poor man.
With this I consider myself king.

Against the pre-dawn light

Against the pre-dawn light,
Socrates walks toward the town square.
My goldfish stops.
I measure myself
against the significant digits
of the slide rule.

The tree Socrates argues with is I.
He will not drink hemlock
for another day.
No, for the dew drops
on the grasses heavily lie,
and for their brevity,
Socrates will die.

Logic and method are useless
in arguing with the pre-dawn sadness.
Go, then, Socrates, go to the town square
and argue with the significant
and the insignificant,
though they conspire to take
your life.

I argue with my father,
his length laps my length,
his reach outspans my reach,
and his hand covers mine.
What measure am I left
in the pre-dawn light?

Socrates will die, it is already known.
My father will die, by logic
and the fact he is mortal.
I look again out the window.
Socrates moves against the pre-dawn light.
And in my room, my goldfish swims again.
I live.

The slide rule is no applicable measure.

Apple moment

I was a snail, I hauled my house
Equidistant from you,
A flower on an apple bough;
And through the sky kaleidoscope,
and from your checkered skirt,
The suggestion of cherry…

Now time has passed and generalized you:
The first kiss, flavored by bubble gum;
The bright red skirt of a flamenco dancer,
And as poppies on the terrace of a private home,
And finally,
As a source of light, in my rented home…

At the bus stop

A young woman peels
herself like a banana,
soft, sweet, and fragile...

Others gawk, seem pleased;
my sole reality is
the chicken I am eating;
my allowance under these political
times is a bus transfer.

She laughs while the cherry trees conspire
to bear fruits;
perhaps the worms quietly sift
soil around their roots;
perhaps the bus moves
across poorer neighborhoods...

She readies her money, zipping
herself back up, creates
a mystery I cannot designate
time or place.
She mounts the bus while I wonder
what to do with my greasy fingers.

An Old hotel dweller

Smoke detectors page me down these halls.
Cooking pork snouts no doubt, my arthritic bones
rickshaw me down scented rugs to the toilet stall.
Old San likes to read old papers and fart alone.
First the check is late, then mice noisily came,
and the daughter moves to another town.
Old photographs and plaster can but come down.
When Old San sneezes, he discovers he's lame
and eight flights of stairs lead down to the snow.
The women in the washroom will only say
may the Virgin Mary give us more hot water.
Old age is like this, Old San has been told.
But I am still living, though life is a bother.
I hope I won't be a putrefying mess on the next rent day.

You naughty woman smiling coyly at me

with your smile curving like a sickle,
and I, a handful of wheat, I am telling you
my requirements are complex, but for now
I'll order a #3 with your smile there,
under the armpit of the waitress, across the room.

The Eskimos offer to their brothers traveling
the wide expanse of cold their wives.
It is a cold day, I am sitting here and your coy
smiles are unknown to your husband, with
the newspaper between the two of you.

My sweet-and-sour pork is tart today.
The Chinese say vinegar is envy and jealousy.
The kitchen is a gong ensemble;
When the cooks go home in nights like bits
of shrimp in bittermelon soup,

Their wives will timidly rub their loins
against them, but they will be asleep.
I live here and the last time I went out
for roast duck with plum sauce, I dined alone.
Thank you for smiling, I am alive under the table.

At the Tokyo Airport

Cold juice, cold Mt. Fuji,
A child alone dining.
Empty plane, empty heart.

Vast auditorium.
Hearing six tourists talk
About America.

Six bites of hot chicken.
Six swallows of cold juice.
Six hours, America.

Child alone, lonely child,
Here, six lotus petals
From Buddha, Mt. Fuji.

Where are your friends, your friends?
Where is your family?
In Buddha's lotus palm.

Man alone, lonely man,
Where lies your loneliness?
In the mist of the world?

Psychoanalysis of a room

Its only window is the eye of Cyclops on the world.

Lamplight of honey, a dusty guitar on the wall.
Many rivers merge behind the bookshelf.
A premature cry gushes like steam in the radiator.
The family screams but the typewriter clicks on.

The mirror accelerates the curvature of the unadorned wall.
Clean sheets achieve a similar effect.
The child learns the power of crayons, while more soberly,
the grown man jots the notation of infinitesimals.

The child is put to bed, his colors symmetric arcs
in the lamplight of honey, while the grown man looks
up to the ceiling and sighs,
for what is he if his principles are refuted by the night
and he is himself reduced to a microscopic groove?

No matter, he goes on with his infinitesimals,
naked, precise, and relentless.
The child sleeps
while the grown man expects a guest who never comes.
In the womb of the night,
the grown man shrinks into the child
with lamplight of honey and a dusty guitar on the wall.

The grown man goes to bed and the world pauses
just long enough for the child to get off.
The child resumes the man's work
and makes the notation of infinitesimals.

In Water Buffalo time

The water buffalo is a black boulder around which white
Butterflies flit, controlling the image of my village.
It is four pillars holding up a shrine topped by Attila's head.
Slapping its paintbrush tail, sure-footed, it advances
Slowly, not impressed by dynastic inventions of paper, compass,
    and gunpowder,
Nor by imperial vassals intoxicating concubines with plum wine.
This working philosopher, benign beast of the East, a prince
Meditating on plum blossoms while the kingdom is overrun
By brigands no different than soldiers.
It sinks its head into the grass on the perimeter of the village
Pond where daggers of carp and dace rip his shadow on the water,
Where black shrimp and loaches scout the bottom
And snails cling to slate banks.

In earliest mornings, I woke to the village dialect jostling
In my head like cauliflowers sizzling in sesame oil
In the wok, like chatty sparrows in the yung tree,
Like cicadas in bamboo groves, like buckets splashing
Into the village well. I heard the drinking song of the men
In the village yard the night before. With bamboo pipes
And a bucket of rice wine, they had sung:

"Heavy, heavy, the dew lies over the clovers.
Bring, bring out flasks of silver.
Merry, merry under a dome of stars.
But soon, too soon this night will be over…"

Voices taut, frog drums deep as rice paddies.
But I dreamt a deeper voice, my father's pales in comparison.
It's hinted by gungfu drums, bellow of water buffalo, a racine fissure.
It was as proclaimed by Lu Hsun, "In the stillness of mountains,
Hear the peal of thunder." But when I woke, the dew was gone.
A shaft of sunlight fell on my childhood slate.

My sister renews the Ming vase with fresh pussywillows.
Grandmother steams rice, and the chicken sits on a new egg.
I drink tea from the spout while my sister redoes my shoelaces.
Off to school 3 li away, trotting on village pond banks
And collecting schoolmates in the morning haze.
When I see a water snake swimming on the lotus pond,
I déjà vu Narcissus lost his life. His gifts came early
And ours not at all. We are the contingent of zodiac animals
Off to seek Buddha: the horse, the rabbit, the tiger, the rooster…
The ox trots out first, faithful, steadfast, but when he
Arrives, the rat on his back jumps off
And gets to Buddha first.

I often meditate at the pond near the school,
Watching the soft, thin legs of the praying mantis
Subdue a bug in full armor, seeing it as the monks did
In Shaolin Temple 500 years before. Other masters studied
The movements of cranes, eagles, and birds fighting with snakes.
Li Po, our legendary poet, in 700 A.D., perfected
The Drunkard's Style of gungfu, which bewilders
The opponent with fluid but erratic movements.

When my little friends mocked me for my seriousness,
Our teacher, under the shade of the yung tree bursting with berries,
Told us Meng-Tse had dreamed he was a butterfly
Dreaming it was a man. I was confused, in a house
Of mirrors, and thought existence is mutual illusion.
Would I cease to exist if I didn't think of my dog
Who thinks of me? My little friends made faces at me.

New Year comes to the village banging a gong
And exploding demon-chasing firecrackers. And lucky money.
But the village recedes away like the galaxies. In these
Thirty years what will not change in form or utility
Except art for its own sake?
Heraclitus says I can't cross the same river twice.
Einstein says if I must I can go to the future, but never to the past.

But surely as long as one water buffalo is fanned by
The evening breeze, the village is there like the smile of the Cheshire Cat
And exists in the Platonic world; all else is an approximation.

Sunflowers, yellow and white chrysanthemums, lychees,
Girls' red cheeks, dew-moist wintermelon little buddhas
In the gardens. Robins, beetles, and cicadas sing my way
To my uncle's village. He rises and his wife burns incense.
He clears the abacus with one motion and teaches me the rhymes
One chants to enable the fingers to go faster than the brain.

He is a wine merchant steeped in Confucius.
Where would a woman wash her husband's clothes
If not at the river by the ancestral shrine?
What part of the chicken to give to the nephew if not the drumstick?
And how else to measure but by exact yards and inches?
He has many children but there is no unnecessary noise.

I forage the pine hills behind his house as a bandit.
The turpentine from the virgin pines makes me dizzy.
The wood is kept as furniture for newlyweds.
I play until I fear real bandits will come
When the sky is devout with thousands of incense tips.

But surely memory is selective. I don't remember not having
My mother's milk, only the quarrels with village women
My mother's age. I don't remember three generations of a family
Taken by dysentary, just the bitter cod liver oil
My grandmother spooned me.
I don't remember my cold little toe except that cloth was allotted
Only once a year, and only in black or blue.
I don't remember famines, just the human chain formed
To relay water to the stricken rice paddies,
Where the leeches had dehydrated.

Still, village girls marry as soon as the dew evaporates
From the corn. The mulberry was for jumping into the village pond.
What China had, we had. And when it was all quiet,
The sunflowers so turned. The papayas got fat and golden,
And peasants trotted out with hoes and straw hats.
It is quiet in the garden where I fish in the pond.
Peas incubate in pods, the lettuce full and clean,
And ladybugs monitor the gardens
To make sure this is the order of things
Before the invention of mail delivery.

In the semi-tropical evening, pink clouds race and diffuse
Like the colors and textures of my jade bracelet.
The water buffalo is led into the dusty village yard,
Mud caked on its loins, distracted by my dog cutting
Across its path. He collects his primeval motions into shape,
Shakes his Hegelian head, exhales, slaps his paintbrush tail,
Lapses into a revery, and goes into internal monologue:

O beast I am, humble beast.
Some man, he must have been an emperor,
Or the son of such an emperor, said, "The Original Son
Is the mother of the universe, the sword that divines light
From chaos, the mother of all things…"

The sun atop the tree is East.
The mountains seek comfort in the hills, the hills seek
Rest in the valleys, and the valleys beget rivers.
The mountain cat descends into the lowlands
And the field mice look up for hawks
And the darkening earth looks for the moon…

And loving the grasses as I have for thirty years,
First owned by one man, then by his son,
While the mountains are unvarying.
With mud caked on my loins, trudging the maze of rice fields,

A black dot against unvarying mountains,
The soil furls, my eyebrows moisten, the bittersweet song
Of my master, himself deep in mud, the fury of work,
Calculating how many bowls of rice the harvest will give.

A beast is not able to calculate mous, catties, and grains.
Work begins when the monsoons recede. In the evening,
When I am sufficiently grazed, I sink into the village pond
And drop dung for black shrimp...

Yet a man, with all his skill on an abacus, is afraid
Of things he cannot see. The man and his family
Are afraid of dark, gloomy gods handed down to them
And buy copious amounts of incense and charms.
My mother, whose teats I suckled for only a brief while,
Gave me no such gods of thunder to fear.

I don't even fear tigers. A man is cursed with worry:
Thieves because he has too much, fires because he is careless,
And ghosts because he offends others.
But I, with the gold-pleated sky for a blanket,
Sweet-smelling rice straw for a bed, a breeze from the river,
I have recompense for my toil, with the village symphony
Of crickets, cicadas, and bullfrogs,
I shall say beasthood is as good as Buddhahood.

I conjecture a water buffalo constellation in another galaxy,
A real spirit, not a tattered array of dying stars,
A form but not only a form.
Up in heaven, my soulmate has no ring pierced
Through his elegant nose and no harness to shackle him down.
And here below, if beasts can speak, we will form quorums
And overthrow empires by a conspiracy of tails.

But alas, nature gives us no such voice or equipment
Just a reluctant compliance to serve.
Though our masters in turn fear the tax collectors,
It is we who are sold, exchanged, or placed on the chopping block.
We do not think? No!
Our lack is that our intelligence is not equal to our strength.

The beast is weary, is led by a boy to a bed of straw.
Inside our house, in the kerosene lamplight,
My sister undoes her ponytail, which a while ago was a bowstring
Back from a political meeting, she says tractors will come
To our village. When electric lamps light up the village yard,
She says, ghosts will be gone.
Grandmother, with her feet bound in the last dynasty, will see
New light with her old eyes.
She gives me crackers and tea, and draws the mosquito net.
I hear a faint moan from the water buffalo.
He too will be liberated.

Though the past is solipsistic, its existence requiring
A mind to behold it, childhood writes indelibly
A million dollar check into life.
Dragonflies hover over chrysanthemums
Like helicopters over a burning forest.
Bananas and grapes bunch together like families.
Women splash buckets into the well.
I look for the faint prints of water buffalo.

The water buffalo got old and died.
It was shared by the whole village,
Lucky money for a calf conscripted.
A sad note crept into the men's drinking songs,
But not for long, with rice wine they sang
Again of subduing tigers and the various calamities
From the beginning of time.
On my childhood slate were drawings of chickens, mulberries,
And numerals from Arabia.
Then I learned how to write the characters "water buffalo."

Egg tarts

Once talking to Maria, she's Greek, worried
About bi-cultural adaptation, asked me
If I like Chinese girl or American, told me
When she doesn't feel Greek, she'll buy baklava.

I squelch diary, querulous birds in hell &
Go to Ten Thousand Things Have Mothers Bakery
While Chinatown rust travels from building
To building, shop to shop.

It's a trick to feel Chinese even in Chinatown
Where tour buses inch along, the driver pointing out
Its exotic features while winos slump,
Street people, tattooed guns and knives,
Benevolent orders tight-lippedly banging

Mahjong. It'd take some articulate she-poet
To slit my bamboo frame: Opaque, hard, and abuse-
Resistant outside, but inside, a cavity,
Flip-flopping to dissonant winds, to needs.

Yellow lights of pagoda lanterns,
Unabashed verses, not wind through sparse bars,
Not winds through bamboo groves,
Papaya-ginger breath, I am not bamboo but arrows.

Now, Maria, I go for egg tarts to feel Chinese.
Little sweet buddhas behind beaded curtains
At 3 A.M., fashioned by Fushi, the god of creation,
Received by yellow hands and minds,
Belly-filling as verses translated from the Tang.

How to cook rice

Measure two handfuls for a prosperous man.
Place in pot and wash by rubbing palms together
as if you can't quite get yourself to pray, or
by squeezing it in one fist. Wash it
several times to get rid of the cloudy water;
when you are too high in Heaven looking down
at the clouds, you can't see what's precious below.
Rinse with cold water and keep enough so that
it will barely cover your hand placed on the rice.
Don't use hot water, there are metallic diseases
colliding in it. This method of measuring water will work
regardless of the size of the pot; if the pot is large,
use both hands palms down as if to pat your own belly.
Now place on high heat without cover and cook
until water has been boiled away except in the craters
resembling those of the moon, important
in ancient times to growing rice. Now place lid on top
and reduce heat to medium, go read your newspaper
until you get to the comics, then come back and turn it down to low.
The heat has been gradually traveling from the outside
to the inside of the rice, giving it texture;
a similar thing happens with people, I suppose.

Go back to your newspaper, finish the comics, and read
the financial page. Now the rice is done, but before
you eat, consider the peasant who arcs in leech-infested
paddies and who carefully plants the rice seedlings
one by one, and this night, you are eating better than he.
If you still don't know how to cook rice, buy a Japanese
automatic rice cooker; it makes perfect rice every time!

Far and near

With the routine and inadvertent sounds of everyday machinery
still around me, I begin to hear faint perturbations from
greater distances. In the moments the ears adjust from near
to far, it is difficult to distinguish between a soft whisper
spoken in the bedroom from the dying breath of something
that has traversed the entire cosmos to reach me. Near or
far — I don't always know the difference: is it some immodesty
an acquaintance is speaking here or is it a great statement
rumbling toward us from a great distance, reaching us as
the breath of an exhausted Aztec messenger?

And my breath upon the bath water, when I have sunk so low
that my nostrils are just above the liquid, will propagate
waves. The waves will reflect from the banks at the far
reaches of the bathtub. I may mistake the reflections for
something that didn't originate with me. And perhaps I will
hold myself perfectly still. When I am perfectly still and
content, above the immediate and magnified sloshing of the
bath water and the drip of the faucet, I will hear my wife
in another room, reading to our child.

A Moment in my rented room

I sometimes think of myself as an astronaut
In my compact, rented room and look upon the bookshelf
With its deep mathematics books for deeper space
As from a voyage one cannot return.
Then multiply by several million men who cannot marry,
Men who cannot own homes, or work, or go to college.
This is almost equal to the space effort.
But why all that money? I can go to Pluto by just
Being in a bad mood.

Sometimes I think of the loneliness of deep space
In my rented room. The neighbors have busily gone off
To Epsilon Centauri or Galaxy X-2137 or to the 7-Eleven.
Sometimes I look at my 16-oz. jar of coffee; I know
What the minimum daily requirements are. Cybernetics
Steers me to avoid collisions with black holes or stars,
And my hot plate sustains me with pinto beans and bacon rinds,
And on my mini-stereo, always the Blue Danube.

It is rainy today. My room is a bastion. I am filing
The sparse bars of prison. I am building a mental atom bomb.
I am designing spaceships. Multiply this by several millions.

Aberdeen, 1966,
or, driving around for a poem

Driving behind a logging truck with dancing flags
Pinned on the logs, I listen to "Norwegian Wood" by the Beatles.
Miss Freeland wants a poem for her creative writing class.
In the pulse of sawmills, I cut this logging town
Into board feet with my '55 Plymouth, with sawdust
Plenty to make ice-cream cones. I tend to forget
The manure that gives us Red Delicious, or this memory.

Between windshield-wiper swings, I hear the tugs' blasts.
Perch and red snapper flap on Scandinavian boats,
Neighborhoods where I sold subscriptions of *Reader's Digest*
In Finnish or Polish editions. Catching a glimpse
Of a girl at the S. H. Kress coffee counter, I think
Of the book on the backseat, *Eleven Kinds of Loneliness.*
The doctors in the antiseptic Backer Building can't take away
This and other pains of a small town.

It is near Xmas. My little brother peeks out the window
Of the car. He is promised hot dogs and ice cream for coming along.
If a pretty girl raises her umbrella, I'll write a long poem.
No such luck. We cross over to Cosmopolis to see
Boys fishing the Wishkah for sturgeon.
The car is damp, the heater doesn't work.
In the monotony of rain and windshield-wiper swings,
I think I have a rhythm to beat the words against.
My brother and I settle for hot dogs and milkshakes
At a drive-in going out of town.

Hank keeps coming back to Aberdeen

Thinking of the hometown is checking the oil stick of the car.
Hank keeps coming back to Aberdeen
With his bare arms in the stickers, to pick Evergreen blackberries,
To find dew-covered, almost empty, slug-aboded beer bottles
     in dead-end streets,
To mow dandelioned lawns for two bits,
To stand on the seat of his moving bike, to bowl, to shoot 8-ball.

Agent orange sky, sulfur in our throats;
The sawmill rips logs into lumber. Pulp, paper mills suck up
     the town's abled;
(Mr. Duffy, the disabled, lived the quiet terror of long afternoons,
     game shows, and Oly's.)

     You see,
Clean air wasn't our class concern;
Povertied minds have no tendril nor palms reaching from
     the end of thought.
My mother steamed the suckers I caught at the slough
     without thought of raw sewage.
We lamented free food being lost in oysters in mudflats,
Dungeness crabs when the immense Pacific surf rolled in,
     black with birds' feathers and baby razor clams.
Hank comes back to reach, bare-armed, into the Evergreen cyclone
     for hand-staining sweet berries.

Often a man

Often a man listens to faraway woods, like a wolf may pause
In snowy shadows for winds that may bring the aroma of bread,
And reflects on the glory and the shame of the pack,
How it hunts and tears flesh from flesh, sips blood from the jugular of
A lamb, and how yet when the pack moves stealthily by a country church
In the moonlight that falls and glides on the frozen fields
To the ailing schoolhouse, their bags unzipping to penciled wisdom
Gleaned between the milking of the cow and blowing out the long candle
In the childhood bedrooms that fill all farmhouses that flock together
For comfort and company, and in their communal pledges,
Erect churches where the pastor says it as best he can...

The man often hears blood in his ears when in his bed alone.
He looks up at the ceiling and he knows he should not be smoking...
The woman, not his, is meticulous and tender, who at this hour is
      anointing her face,
Which is already beautiful, her curls dangling at her temples,
The skin smoother than the skin of grapes, in soft whispers she calls
The name of the man she loves but they have never met...
He is a singer who moves across the stages of the world,
More famous than Russian poets or political leaders,
He croons just three words and young girls swoon; he lines his guitar case
With drugs and contraband goods, exits with the brutal custody of bobbies,
And the woman, no longer a young girl, knows everything about the singer,
And in the late hour, when snow threatens to fall on farmhouses,
She flicks on the bed lamp and reads the magazine of famous people,

Forgetting altogether the dreary hours at the checkout stand of
    the large variety store
Where she's a cashier, pennies go with pennies, and five dollar bills
    with five dollar bills.
All the while the man who often hears blood throb in his ears
Dreams about five numbers straight across, a pack of Old Gold cigarettes,
And is wondering about the feasibility of a hamburger at Jack-In-The-Box
At this hour…

A wolf too may listen to a man when a man is happy and is
    strumming a guitar
Like the water of six rivers, the wolf too may sing as a beast can
After he steals the oil of sanctuary lamps and forgets about
    childhood shame,
He wanders over sweet grasses and white barley, his nostrils moist
And filled with the aroma of bread that rises from the chimneys
    of farmhouses
In little villages, out of which little boys and girls walk
Into hospitals and company-owned gift shops, or go as high as the lectern
Of a state-run university, while the man with the blood throbbing
    in his ear,
The woman reading the magazine in bed have never met except,
    unknown to each,
He hands her a dollar for a lottery ticket, and she's very happy
At that precise moment because, over the music system of the store,
They are playing a song of the singer she loves…

The Inadvertent persuasion of a rented room, or, the evolution of context...

She, a deviant psychotic who used to ride with bikers, a big tattoo of a peacock on her thigh, played chess against the philosopher-counselor. In the opening, I saw he was ahead with a knight or bishop, which he captured and put next to his tobacco pouch on the dining room table. I went back to the editing of the halfway house newsletter, *The Trying Times,* fancying myself to be a great molder of the therapeutic opinions of the institution of which I was a member, facilitating work- or school-congruent attitudes at the expense of the government and private charities.

Later, when I looked up to the dining room clock, an hour had passed. And I remember now, quite strangely enough, how Franz Kafka wrote in a passage that he was in a frantic, confused hurry in the town square, and he didn't know what time it was. He asked the policeman stationed there, with great beseeching. You know how exaggerated Kafka writes. The policeman, quite out of character of being a helpful person, said, "And from me you wish to know the time?" Back to the chess game, it appeared the girl had won. I asked the philosopher if there wasn't some mistake. He forlornly said the result is the truth, and that he had played badly although he started out well. Earlier he had engaged us in a discussion of "The Elephant Man," an actual historical figure who had to wear a mask at all times in order to avoid frightening people with his ugliness.

Years later, after we had graduated from successful living at the psychiatric halfway house, I ran into Anita on the street downtown. It appeared she hadn't eaten much in days, and so with what little money I had, we had cake in a downtown department store cafeteria. It became evident she was paranoid still, she told me she had just been released from the hospital. She described in very odd ways the way furniture was arranged in the ward to persuade certain therapeutic methods of thinking. She also described the way they talked to her gently but firmly about rules, especially getting out of her room. She thought it was an intrusion into her freedom of movement. The psychiatric authorities said it was to help her to adjust and get along in the world, for eventual return to employability.

I was on my way via bus to clarify something with a writer in another district of the city. I invited Anita to come. She became quite agitated and evasive, finally divulging that certain people there were trying to kill her. Totally illogical of course, she should simply move to another town if that was true, and if it was true, it'd also mean they'd be looking for her. Yet, in all her madness, she didn't think I was an agent they hired to entice her to go there, or that I was a simple assassin. Perhaps she reasoned that it would create too big of a public notice if I shot her downtown. Later, as we were going out of the multi-million dollar shopping complex, she eluded me by claiming to go to the bathroom and vanishing through a different door. I haven't seen her since.

I don't know what brings her to mind after some ten years. These days I don't watch television or listen to the radio, and seldom find interest in the newspapers. I've returned to my old love of philosophy, and wonder about the philosopher who substituted those couple of weeks at the halfway house and who went to a prison and worked as a counselor, and I muse now myself that in chess, nothing is hidden except the mind.

A Slow ox-cart hauls the sage; his robe is opened to the wind

Such a slow journey, cats will sleep,
The Western Capitol will change hands.
Out with beggars, the sage sees red
Apples whose insides are rotting
While the outside remains fair;
The sage sees the nation as
A well-armored bug in late fall,
Who, if a wind blows him on his back,
It is the end. Going from gate to gate,
The sage knocks lightly, so as
Not to disturb the entertainment there.
When granaries deplete to feed mounted
Archers, and song and dance crescendo
Inside imperial walls, it is time for
Beggars to go begging; the slow ox-cart hauls
The sage, his robe is opened to the wind.
Ruffians intimidate the weak and the poor,
And in the dead of the night,
An arrow is shot at the emperor's door.

"Fortune telling..."

How sometimes in graveyard hours,
In the kitchen of our Chinese American restaurant,
All lights flicked off save one naked bulb, sitting at a makeshift
table, sitting on milk crates,

How my father, in his soft green sweater,
Now softened by age and grudgingly recognized by his competitors,
Which are other Chinese American restaurants, pizza parlors,
Mexican restaurants and the like,

Now it's 3 A.M. The walk-in refrigerator hums a forlorn
tune, what a hobo sometimes hears of the rails humming...
    We have finished eating, after the whole town has eaten.
In the necessary fury of work, we have overlooked our simple needs.
    He repeats his story: build your future on the foundation
of your forebears; that someday I am to understand; now the light
from the naked bulb is frazzled and somewhat eerie,
but there's really no need to turn on all the white lights
of the kitchen, and after all, there's only us here, and we can
talk in the dark without losing comprehension,
even without looking at each other...

How my father, his back curving more each year
From the weight of the morning air,
The ever-increasing weight of wife and eight children,
All permissable dreams and sorrows clinging on like grapes,
That in the unofficial histories of his veins,

Bombs dropped near his village, metal and body parts flew;
The naked bulb here was the same naked bulb in Angel Island,
detained there because he was an immigrant, a Chinese immigrant...

How his back would arc more,
That over forty years he bent over the wok,
The only use of his curved back now is to use it as a bow,
Like the bow of William Tell,
Take his children and grandchildren,
They are arrows,
And from his curved back,
Shoot them toward the stars....

This is a romantic story.
He died young, labored away his time rather than love.
And consequently he accumulated money.
His oldest son,
Whose mind was mended by electric currents,
Has a receptive mistress in every town,
He visits every town as a salesman.
The competitors are awed by his powers of persuasion,
And grudgingly admit his gift,
But first they isolate his history from all other histories...

48

How my father was buried
In the same cemetery as Bruce Lee. I am not comparing heroes.
My father was not a hero.

His grandfather was another immigrant from another century
to these same lands, when rails were young.
My father admired the blood of his precursors, going back
to the dawn of man, and their blood is in his blood,
their history his history,
And so my father tells his oldest son:
"Consider the foolish man who tells an ox to climb a tree…"

How my father lives again in the Chinese American kitchen,
In the mind of the oldest son,
Whose mind is mended by electric currents,
Who could not speak for vacant decades,
As entropic grasses grow over cemeteries,

But here is the Chinese immigrant,
A stooping figure among the sacks of onions, vinegar, and bittermelons,
A yellow lemon contained entirely by its rind,
And people, and after a while, his own children
don't like the same rice, the same telling of those histories,

Because beneath worlds of sugar and love,
There are basic routines.
The father who told of his grandfather,
Who told of opium in China,
That for the peace it gave, a man his daughters sold…

The Woman in the next room

Has a craving for a banana
And is convinced I am a spy after her secret.

She's reading one of those paperback books where
The heroine leads a successful double life.

She works in a doctor's office
And she flies to Florida once a year to read

A book in this next hotel room
And is worried about the minimum upkeep of a spy

Which I am. I know she rinses her lettuce
Many times and she has a secret kept in a semi-

Precious gem box no one can see or open.
She is slender and naked upon the hotel bed

Just reading while the potted ferns tremble
Because someone has closed a door down the hall.

We come to this hotel once a year and live
In two adjacent hotel rooms and I pretend

I don't know her and she wants me to call her
On the telephone and talk to her about stocks and real estate.

It's all I've got, he said...

The light rain, he said, and the occasional let up's all I've got,
And walking around the block's an adventure then…

He used to write poetry, went surf fishing, my one line tossed into the ocean,
He said, is all I can do, now at night the phone cord slips like a snake
Into underworld catacombs…

I used to chop at Whitman's block of wood, he said, but I cannot gallop
Like Robert Frost, even walking in the woods you would pick up some dirt,
And since no woman would, himself he caressed and said, it's all I've got…

He used to know the seasons' birds and the afterglow of the summer sun in meadows,
Now he reads Anne Sexton and is no longer concerned if the soul survives;
The other day I looked through the peephole of a construction site,
He said, good people will no longer live in houses of wood,
High in the tower, they will try to prove the existence of dirt.

In San Francisco in my torrid hour, he said, when Hamlet's soliloquy was about me,
An old poet came to see me and said, Africa's darkest troubles are caused by diamonds,
Which last forever…

He said, I'm tired of talking. Can we walk around the block? Here are the dandelions
And the weeds that push their way through the cracks of the sidewalk,
A solitary dandelion sometimes showers in its yellow gold,
Its bloom many times brighter than the sun.
It's all I've got, he said…

The Spy's reliability...

He was at the corner donut shop; that was his assignment. He watched
the donut-maker Buck and the chess players, in particular the Iranian
chess master; the other hangers-on, the drug dealers and so forth were
only of minor importance. He comes in the day, ostensibly to play chess
and talk about psychotherapies. At night he comes, ostensibly to read a
book on economics by Samuelson. Everyone knows he is a spy, however,
since most of them are spies themselves, and it takes one to know one,
as the saying goes. The Fillmore District was full of spies, because the
newspapers were all printed there, in all the languages that were popular
in the city...

He plays chess sometimes in off-hours at night, and on weekends when
he pretends he can't sleep in his rooming house nearby, he comes to see
Buck, to play chess and say his school books are driving him crazy.
He purposely loses to Buck, a black guy who never really had time to
study chess, and Buck will feel good and whisper things to him, that
there's saccharine in the donuts in place of sugar, and that this little
donut shop is really owned by a black church, not the little black guy
they called Steve. The spy never seems to be prying. He always seems to
be unimpressed, so that Buck tells more and more, juicier and juicier
tidbits, hoping to make him happy...

The spy himself has had no communications with command for a
long time. There could have been changes in the command structure or
channels of communication, breakdowns, paralysis due to infiltrations
by hostile forces, or just an inadvertent oversight, meaning he is lost in
the paperwork. Or, the most satisfactory explanation to him, he is so
deep in the bowels of the investigation that he is miles under the ground,

beneath the beds of rivers and dinosaur fossils, so close to the fire itself that they don't dare jeopardize his cover...

The Iranian chess master plays the other players blindfolded, ten at a time, while smoking imported Iranian cigarettes. He of course has no chessboard; he just shouts his moves, the mind is all. The other players play him for money and they smoke Marlboros and Camels and Kents and drink coffee and eat saccharine donuts at all the little tables in the Fillmore and Vallejo donut shop while cars go in four directions outside, and occasionally a thug-thug teenaged music car slouches around the street corner slowly, like Yeat's Beast in his metaphysical poem to be reborn. The Iranian loses all ten games, and pays the money that has been wagered. It seems the money has petroleum stains on it. The spy makes a note of this...

Usually, unless one's a mole, a spy is to be transferred frequently so that his objectivity and consequent usefulness is not jeopardized by inadvertent and undesirable attachments to his subjects. So, since the spy hasn't been notified of any transfers, in fact, has had no communications whatsoever, he begins to think his cover has been blown, in a deep and profound way that could damage the entire apparatus, and more and more, he comes to the unattractive but forced conclusion that he's been written off, forgotten and abandoned, and therefore he is free at last, to see what he sees without a fixed format of interpretation, to simply live among the people as if they were his brothers and sisters. It is difficult to say which is the cause and which is the effect, the net result is that when Buck asks him to play chess, he says yes. He's no longer reliable...

53

THE MORRISON

1993 – 1996

I Have augmented my premise of isolation and sorrow: the world comes into the pallor of my room...

Mi compadre, everything of importance comes into the pallor of my room,
Like furtive sunlight when I take a furtive look, pushing back the drapes.

Water comes into my room, and it is backed by the city reservoir,
And backed by the sky itself, virtually infinite in scope...

And today there's a gray sky over the gas chamber outside my window,
And why do I feel the fear of 10 years ago, when Vincent Chin's head was

Bashed in by a Michigan baseball bat, as I try to be judicious
About jalapeno, garlic, oolong tea, and tempura, and how do they differ,

And how are they the same? It took 10 years and the destruction of
6' x 4' x 4' or 96 cubic feet of poetry and 10 years to make me feel better,

And I have now moved into a bigger room, room enough to blues
     the guitar,
Have now room for Nietszche and Immanuel Kant on a corner bookshelf,

And now my phone calls someone and that someone calls someone
     and so on...
And now I can reach the White House oven indicator light,

And so I've retreated from many many premises in my life but I'll
Retreat no more, because my psychiatrist said, "People are
     jumping off bridges,

This is a city of paved streets, and it takes a city 300 years
to have its buses run on time…"

And in 300 years, the garbage dumps will be archeological sites,
And all the glory of our civilization will be carefully examined

By our children's children, but no temples or roads will remain,
Only the subterranean songs that flow in the people's veins…

There is a world I am...

Whether it is this world's tomorrow,
Or another world's today,
There is a world I am in the machinery of the infinite,

Whereas some shapely tenement woman makes the "o" sound,
When frightened by mice coming too close to the candle,
When the fuse governing the city's electricity is blown...

And when I see her human face over the alphabet soup she ladles
In the ho-hum of a slow existence behind the workman's counter,
I know I will pull her from the elevator,
While my typewriter is in fast idle,
Awaiting impatiently the rhythmic slams of the carriage return...

There's more than a third of the world in the Third World,
Where self-augmenting is the word while the words augment themselves
Elsewhere, where civilization is theft and word thieves meet book thieves
Over a New York steak and talk long and thin
In the empty restaurant;

While I sleep under the statue across the street, waiting
For this world's tomorrow, or another world's today...
Waiting for the machinery of the infinite, for a world of inadvertent sounds,
A world in which I am...

The **Wind** is gentle on my forehead...

Going to the hills of October,
The wind gentle on my forehead,

The wine and sisters of friends
Light up these copper hills;

An insect falls from my cupboard
Among the ketchup, soy sauce, garlic,

Coffee filters that smooth my skin,
Lulling me to the belief —

A massacre of a million is always
Somewhere else, and how else

Should I think? That I am a criminal
Because mankind is a criminal

And I didn't say so? The three lines
On my forehead are the trigram for "wind"

And "gentle" like the cool October wind
On the forehead after a night of

Torrid reasoning. Give me this chemistry,
Give me, Eileen my love, intoxicate me,

For I cannot wake up: I wake from one dream
Only to be dreaming again of you,

Twenty-four years later. A gentle wind is blowing
On my forehead. I am soothed by your palm.

Yes, there is a slight fever, my love;
There is a slight fever, indeed!

In my room...

In my room the world is true
Simply because I say it is true,
And truth is "spread out, like a patient,
Etherized upon a table..." in many rooms,
Rooms like mine...
And if you come to my room, one of the many
Parallel rooms that connect like the sections
Of a dragon, one black and one golden,
Interwoven and locked in mortal combat...
And in which room with a couch,
A man writes in the air with his index finger,
And the heads of the two dragons peer into this room,
And that's when the shooting starts,
Below the window of the third floor,
In the streets below.
And in my room you appear without a summons,
And the many parts of the mind
Assemble themselves here,
And I touch your hair,
You turn and smile
In this room, a room that is so similar to,
And yet so different from all the other rooms,
Simply because you have entered,
And suddenly more than one mind contemplates the rose,
Not here, but where they do such things...

Here, the only thing real is
What you say is real, Eileen,
And you ask, "Will there be an operation?"
And operations of various kinds have been going on
In these rooms for years,
And the operator says, "Let the Tao move the scalpel"
And do not assert or proclaim the current coffee,
Nor any flags on ships that transport grain,
Because what one hungry world wants and one solitary room needs
is love, love for all the rooms in this similar class,
And rooms that will fill all the spaces of the universe
not already occupied by atoms...

This modal logical moment...

The guitar, its notes falling as a fountain in Spain
Modeled in tape, and bearing the agitated humming from the typewriter...
Know: life is not forever...
As the wind and water softly whisper a record on the beach sand
to say my life was not among the favored,
and the enormous numbers I bet on with a slide rule
Also did not come in at the rail...
And now you are afraid of my anger, because I rip the calendar off,
For over a half of my life I did not search in the right places for you,
Though you saw me all the time as a hapless Bohemian
who sees one tree and asks, "Where are the other nine?"
And goes into a forest as one tree and becomes lost...
And now I type into the typewriter this:
The four corners are illuminated, and this room is a great
     philosophical inquiry,
Catch the light in a rented home.
We have our allotment of bugs and mice,
And in a coin-operated universe such as this one,
It is possible to punch the wrong item,
And there could be some faulty wiring,
And you may not get what you want, if you get anything at all.
But be my friend for this evening;
I am lonely and time spreads itself languidly on the bed,
A rented room somewhere but not far from the tracks,
And you briefly come into it, and Unknown stealthily seeps in,
Pretending to be wind...

I need your presence in this room; it is a good room;
And I am doing good in this room, as Lucifer in his way hangs onto
His corner of Hell, and all the events in the Universe are chained,
And this is a possible room you may have passed through,
     and it could also be
A necessary room for you to stay, and it is not necessary and
     not possible that
It is perfect. No, it is a lit room, and a typewriter is at one corner...

A Moment ago I meant to tell you...

— after J. Seifert

A moment ago I meant to tell you...
It was a ship which brought a storm ashore;
But it is not important now.
    I managed the night fine without you, but the day —
The day is another matter; it goes emptily on and on...
        I read a magazine; I might as well have been reading a piece of
stale bread, or the grime in the sink...
There's something, a great matter that the ship brought in
    just before it burst into flame...

Don't look any longer; don't look anywhere for it;
    Look for it in my face:
        See how the shock turns into a grimace for a moment?
That was a moment ago... it is not here now!
A moment ago I wanted you to touch my face...
But just then a ship ran aground and burst into flames
    and lit up the night... See? Nobody is sleeping now.
How can they?
    A moment ago you touched my face...

The **Love** this abode contains...

We have lived in 32 abodes, Susanna, red brick, four square,
Nearly a palace, or 32 pages of thin paper, a small book,

And in each story, there's an abode of red brick, inside
Which are a set of 32 books, and the love each book contains

Is more solid than red brick, and four squares together make
A foundation, and so, Susanna, why did you say our love

Cannot exist in paper or fenced by red brick, and is that why
You sold jewelry because you were convinced it was good jewelry,

And stamped visas because we needed more investments in Hong Kong?

Now I'm alone in a single abode of wood and iron nails,
And lone and lonely the cold air seeps and my pen fails,

And, Susanna, where are you since the hospital in 1993?
Should I print your last name and shame your father, who took you

Out to drink with his buddies on the eve of the Chinese New Year?
And you wanted to know if I could get SSI if I went with you

To PSU? Where I would live and you would annotate my mishaps
In your sociology book; and I would tell you everything about

"Michelle," the woman you were so jealous of, and asked me
Is it true. It's half true, Susanna, and only half, for half of us

Live in abodes of paper and half of us live in abodes of brick,
And where the truth is, Susanna, is underneath your left breast,

Where you let me put my right palm in the hospital, because
That's where your heart is...

In the slowness of days...

In the slowness of days I learned the power of soap,
How to formulate a consumable plan on the stove,
And the domesticity of dishes on the counter...

And as the coffee drips, the bare bulbs glare down
Because my lunch is Spartan, and my boots are surplus combat,
And Beethoven's martial music is beating its way

Out of the cabinet which confines it...

And the machine-gun click of my typewriter, Eileen,
And all the endurance of slow days non-punctuated
By ginger or garlic because only enough money for onions...

And the soy sauce is brooding dark, and salt is cheaper
By the pound, and may truth be revealed that in slow days
And slow ways I have always loved you best...

And the television faces every point on the wall by the bed,
And the opposite wall contains a cabinet for my meds,
And boxes of notes, as noted by the government inspector...

And I do not know, Eileen, why I am anxious and nervous today,
Despite the fact we made love not long ago on these premises,
And our voices kiss and caress each other's ears down to the loins,

Daily since the world began. Because in the slow crossing
Of existence, if I do not see my friends, I have gone into
The next room, and so, my love, let's never be separated

In different chambers of the heart, let us journey together
From the center of love to the extremities of fingertips and toes,
And come back as our courage flows like red, red blood,

In the slow crossing of days we do not grow weary or waxed.
In the slowness of days we will blare like the bolero,
And weave and repeat our love in the slowness of days, of all days!

The Last time I got out...

There was no bicameral dichotomous mind the last time I got out
    of the bin,
The snowflake was a snowflake, and the thought of the snowflake was
    the thought of it,
It was simply cold reality, and no matter how much I am sexually attracted

To mannequins in store windows, reality was hard, and hard it comes…

The logical conclusion has to be: Someone is looking at the cold facts
    of cold cash
The wrong way, and it was not me,

For wherever there's money, the world is busy,
As in wherever there's honey, the bee is busy,

And women can smile and men can get hard about cold cash,
And all over thieves and lawyers discuss contraband and private stash…

This time as I left the hospital with $25 for a cab and a hot lunch,
I had no bicameral dichotomous mind,
It was all due to the courtesy of the police,
And the ambulance who had to keep busy,
And the high rises in this city that dwarf and keep the hospital hidden,
And it is not listed or advertised in the phone book,
For a revolutionary in a tenement nook.

This time it was not for simple crooks,
Nor for all the fizz in Manhattan,
Nor for all the piss in China,

This time it was for the way I live,
The way I had to live,
And there were no zen verbal tricks,
For I was born in a house of red bricks,
And I came halfway around the world to live in a house of wood,
Then the sheriff took me outside and in the snow I stood...

A homeless man has a homeless mind,
Because that's the way he has to live,
And no powers will give,

And so across Man's boundless mind he roams,
And never, never finds he a rightful home...

INTERNATIONAL TERRACE

1996 – 1998

At #1105; December 3, 1996

The peace within an underheated, empty room;
the pensiveness of café noir & a Galois cigarette at age 21,
already deemed too old for dueling;
a writing pad, such as this one, while sprawled on a sleeping bag,
deep into the cold house, the cold airs of thought…

Now 26 years later, knowing the "in-between,"
and all the "biting-into-wood" silences of exiles in rooms such as this one,
underheated and undermanned against chaos
seeping in, time and time again;
this has to be my life, Eileen,
knowing the wistful air, the solitudes,
as well as the uncontrollable swellings of the breasts,
the air gushing forth,
the bitter tongue,
& the burn of red peppers,
& the hunger, always the hunger…

Untitled

Today the sunlight is benign as my room is already heated by
    Susie the goddess of electricity...
My ongoing illness for two decades now is taking a benign turn,
                            sweet reprieve, and peace,
And partly it is due to you, and to my taking a course, that it is easy,
    and benign, and nurturing,
And I want to do good...   My coffee, sufficiently hot and eye-opening,
And the steam from the mug holds up the air...
Flight was the return to a room, a room facing the general direction
Of the morning when I rise;
And there's already fame in between these two rooms,
But there was a lot of rain   in between   sunny days...
      And the goodness of whales returning to drowning sailors;
And so we shall find salvation,
Alms, and hunger appeased,
And do not turn around now, someone is entering the room,
That someone will stand at the door and listen to the clicking
    of the typewriter
And listen for the spaces between words,
The silences between this world and its next step,
And the benign, to compose an inhabitable room,
One with a typewriter,   like this one,
And a mug of hot coffee,

The sunlight laminated through the blinds,
    casting a shadow at once dark and unique
Against a pale wall, a pale fire,
The visitor nods a silent encore...
                And tick, tick, click goes the typewriter

I've heard the Chan bells of the monastery...

I've known the valor of underheated, intrepid rooms
    the wistful air, the undernourished underside protected
by the midnight disappearances of the thirty spokes of the wheel...

      And it is in this land that I first knew courage
in the piano hands of a bag lady
                   and I am blurred as to
What's coming squarely down on me like a piano box
in the twisted boots
    the mannequin looks of druggies
                   And the empty roar
of bellows
And what's more
What's more
Are the "urinating multitudes" of headless vagrant bands
    one-meal from death
In the door of the knives,
            one-meal from death
And in this urgent twilight I heard
The bells of the Chan monastery
           And the fog clears
And I am lined against the wall
    facing six long rifles
And instantly I awake
And human voices wake me
"we drown..."

The Solitudes...

"One-heart" is a purple-glazed flag flapping
    and where did the train leave me?   Lately, now, my friend,

I feel the ice, and ice-cracking in the extremities of fingertips
    that hit these typewriter keys
        and leave my thoughts...
I have been among you, my friends, for 35 years —
        in snow, in fog, in rain, in sleet,
As if the mail must get through...
    And I remember you as the sweet viola strings from my native land...
But I had   my solitudes   my slow hours in dingy cafés
    in cypress groves,   in stream beds
and now the cold pristine currents flow in my cranium
        and my warm flesh swells to the music
And pound for pound   There's more of me now!

Focus on the river...

Focus on the river,

           the fisherman seems to continually move upstream...

Focus on man, history seems to forever move downstream...

Therefore, the Tao,

        the Tao says the boat moves because the river moves,

        the fish moves in a moving river,

        but I am still because the banks are still...

Focus on the woman and she'll blush and swell in happiness;

Focus on the ox and he is a black dot on the rice fields,

Focus on the dot and you enter the Tao,

The immutable within the mutables,

           And therefore, a man focuses slightly above his nose

And what he knows is knowledge,

Knowledge of the river,

And of the fish, the smallest of all fish...

Missingness...

To be missing   is devoid of coffee   cold
                                and a cigarette butt
from the discussion of last night
                and the underheated old house
I wasn't there
                but an unfolded piece of paper
spells your identity
                        as you cross the border from one half of the room
to the other half
                        caring less for social convention than before
                                and do not say any familiar phrase
be as off-beat as possible
                        and write out your anxiety on notepads...
        the why's of tomorrow

                                        stale in one day
time that is   is all there is
                                and the inner-city rhythms
give way to dampness
                        under armpits that you
how you wish it were the crotch instead
                                but you could do without it
This is the minimal man
                                the missing   man; man alone
in cold rooms   where a phone is on the floor

And you write your anxieties out
And wonder about reality
And the managed growth
Of your hair   of the city parks   of high rises
         you simply wish   you were missing   somewhat unshaven
with a bowl of chop suey   or a piece of cold pizza
The surface is simple enough   you do not know reality
but the pretense is that you do
                  and perhaps you don't but feel it
like straddling the cracks of an earthquake...

Untitled

Perhaps it is not needed to look beyond coffee as coffee
   As something   bitter   something awakening you   to bitterness
But first coffee as coffee
          the dark liquid, a dark flavor, a bit on the whole unpleasant.
Something you have grown used to,
                of high mountains, the Andes, the vultures,

the pitiless sun…

Anchor yourself against its dark, brooding color, yet its sway

is sharp and refreshing
Coffee as coffee   color as color
              life as life   pain as pain

These pains   This disconnectedness
            where lies my precariousness? Where is the match
that would sparkle the entire terrain?
   And these pains, petty in scope,
            illusioned against a big landscape…
As needles   enter the fabric
             the weaving of your life,
These pains, the experiences of life
        enter the etcetera of your skin   and come in
Into your cosmology   illusioned against the sky

And the only necessary reply   is:

"I was not well..."

As deep as the Pearl I slept, for 36 years, and six assassins in six tries,
    from my native city Canton

Will get anyone, as my mathematics say,

And when my philosophy professor asks me about the Tao,

I can only say, "Sir, it overall returns to the main."

As the veins and arteries

    form a network, and all the capillaries engorge with breath and blood,

And life stamps and steams like a horse

    outside the ale house and is gone with the lighting

of the lamps...

You will relax into this poem as you'd be pleased to expect nothing

You will be pleased to expect a new layer of skin
    as I face friends and foes alike

                        in the double-crosses of crooked roads
        in the ordinary
travels   in a day   taking you to the
                            feeble thoughts
        of daily consciousness
and so let your toes go dead   let the ankles go limp
          let the calves sleep   and paralyze thighs and hips

you do not need all this heavy machinery now
          for you want to relax into poem, into sleep…

The day has been extraordinary hard
          for danger was carried by each car on the street
and every tenth mind   is lethal   and

                   you might meet it anywhere…

    waiting for the bus at a deserted street
            or at a counter that serves chimney soot

and square faces and rough hands objectify you

          but never mind, relax your abdomen, exhale

exhale the stagnant air of cities
       and dream of stars   with the heart   and keep your neck

above the water… let your head ascend, be lighter, lighter than the cares

    of charity, be lighter and travel farther, and float, float away…

So, now as you enter this poem, and finding a drinking fountain

       that leads through water

To the Master of Water, the keeper of archives,

      turn your stereo down, turn down the volume of anxiety,

         like two pips of an apple

and tune in, turn on, and drop out…

    When you wake, it will be fine, but it's been thirty years…

Never mind!
      Give it all up,   take your $5 bills and take your pennies
and start anew… start by
         relaxing into this poem…

In the onslaught of the inadvertent a machinery...

Twenty blackbirds on snowy mountains, the arrogant bard,
Or, twenty times the development of Japan in twenty years?
Now that machinery replaces missionaries,
and I have lost so many poems, written even, typed with the rhythm
of an inner-city typewriter, a gift from a family who bought a navy toilet...

And pound for pound you cannot outfight a Mongol
Who sucks the blood of his horse when the grass is sparse...
And a man's room is not for a woman, while a house or home is,
But where and when shall such good fortune come,
As it is unjustly in favor of those who play along and violate the rules,
And that's why the gods punish Sisyphus...

And now there is harmony as forces bang against each to meter a few words,
that it is better to do that than to mutter a curse...

It is going now, the long going, and how can we go?
Go where you can live forever, though you have only the absolute minimum...
That's simplicity, that's mathematical elegance,
and with it, your empire will live forever, for you have constructed
a house that cannot be seen
and a "horse that eats no grass, and is swift and obedient,"
And the writer goes out for a walk hungry, but for now
"Swallows clouds" and feels light-headed as he pulls the cold iron
of the mailbox and drops this note,
Which he hopes will save another bamboo slit by Li Po,
As the rapid water drowns them in a swift, downward water,
    out to the Yellow Sea...

Sometimes you just have to stop talking...

The failure is not a river you've fished
    where ripe mulberries have dropped...
        And the silk we've spun in our village
Is enviable on damsels of the city...
                        Now, you know what poetry

Essentially is: it is the communication
                of pain

And the most monstrous construction
          is yet to begin
And how like electrons bumping electrons in a strand of copper wire
    that the cars on the freeway
To the left
       of my 11th floor highrise window
Below the hit of hills   and above the grumbling
     of warehouses in the demise
And you always lose money
Trying to keep the truth within bounds
          and as the two-sectioned bus makes
A wide turn   forty private cars follow
High towers flash in the distance
     and a bridge ascends like an on-ramp into infinity
Going to West Seattle
Where a politics of indifference resides
And the light industrial haze rises, rises but vision can still penetrate
Several miles

#1105, now a year later...

Whatever the language, theft seeps into the public domain,
And I write to you of the rain now falling on the kingdom;
That it falls equally on palaces and vacant lots;
On doorknobs of silver and doorknobs of copper...

And the longer the civilization, the longer its corruption
Of ancient texts, of the hinges on tombs, and while today a lamb
hangs in the butcher's window, tomorrow
It might very well be a dog...

And with this long view of things, I can see beyond the hills
Surrounding this part of Seattle that used to be mudflats...
And now an industry of mindlessness is built on violence
In this neighborhood where the police are not helpful...

That's why it rains...
In China, we say, "When it rains, Heaven is answering..."
And Heaven is straight up, but laden with treasures,
You will go straight down!

As the night is beginning to focus...

As the night begins to focus   outside my window
        the cranes of the day   lowering the sky
and the train of cars on rail and on the freeways
        taper as smoke from factories call it a day...
            And the high flying flag is now limp
As if the nation itself will soon close down
And the buses are lack   a   dai   sical   now   for some late
commuters
And the streams of cars are of consciousness
                                        now forgetting

And I smell how the roast in the oven
is darker by degrees
                        and will be fit for serving
When I am done typing
            but why do I type at this hour
When I should be watching the tv news like someone watching
a pair of socks hung to dry
            the grime in the sink can sit overnight again
And these cars   a straight line of them   going presumably home
And home is where I am   saving the steps rolled out from the rug
To the market   for tea leaves
And the electric tram sails   a blur of engines
And the wars going elsewhere will be in the darkest part
of Africa today as the night begins to focus
And someone buys a fat diamond because they are marrying
And so the darkest troubles are forever...

I Want you to write secretly...

I want you to write secretly of secret things,
This I can help you with, the dense sorrows
of the nests of bees, the myriads of ants,
and secretly placing these sorrows
in hearts yet uncorrupted, this I can help...

And write of the lilies on the scum,
the prostitutes in pre-dawn Chinatown,
And the solitary walk of the Canton policeman
through alleys so that the truth is not denied him
From the garbage after a torrid night...

And I want you to read of a mama's concern
from the face of a child,
the intoxication from a broken cup,
and of the great slaughter from three drops
of blood on the butcher's sawdust floor.

Got eyes? The truth comes in like unpaid bills;
Got ears? The lies will be loudly prefaced as truths.
But see what you see, hear from the wall of noise,
As long as you guard your senses,
News comes in as the tingling of bells...

The Relish in the mundane...

The red rays at the end of the day shine like fire
                                  on the white plum blossoms,
and in the mundane, the air is
        dirtier,   the sunsets are
                          more bloody, and life is unfair to you,
my schoolgirl…

But genius has its use someday!
I woke with my heart fluttering because in my dream
            I've run up a long stairway to you,
my heart beating wildly, and now it is morning and I sit alone,
Coffee is not coffee, typewriting is not typewriting
                but the Poe surcease of sorrows hidden in the words
that have flown…

And in Russia, the men dash their glasses and cry "Bitter! Bitter!"
at weddings, and here the smoke rises from industrial chimneys,
and at once
                the city sector is illumined by an early sunrise,
the precocious genius of the day,
And the unbearable optimism begins again
And all the rampant turbulence
of heart
The rush of a lily   toward the unfolding of a family tapestry
toward the expansion of light
                                light as light
the recompense of a night without fire…

Sometimes when I leave behind the places I've been...

Sometimes when I leave behind the places I've been,
A series of cheap hotels, an empty bed smelling of cheap cologne,
the darkest of my first uncle's real estates,
a hot-plated hotel room, up many rickety stairs,
with mice under the washbasin and prostitutes out in the hall,
with photos of a family in Peru and a tongue
unable to distinguish "l's" and "r's,"
finding citizenship a mile away from this den of poverty,
where a thousand Chinese bachelors,
tired of the Chinese newspaper,
loiter in Plymouth Square
or hide in clubs to bang mahjong tiles…

When I leave behind, in roach-scattered tenements,
these separate realities which bounce off my thoughts,
like playing ping-pong alone with the table pushed against the wall,
and now I am given a high-rise apartment in Seattle,
overlooking the water so deep and blue,
my thoughts aren't all that expectant,
just a feeling of validation,
as the tea stain verifies a cup of tea,
and lightly now the traffic down below,
and the muted growth,
nevertheless, like the volume of the world,
filters in, flies in…

Asleep on the floor...

The warm oblivion,
the answer to a night of delirious medication
on the eleventh-floor floor,
the car prowl alarm
like the high-school alarms I slept through
until the train roared through the dew of blackberry vines,
across the dirt field from the old house,
now twenty-some years in memory
staring at a sheet of yellow paper.

The air is warm and thick,
lays me down like anesthesia, and waking, thick-brained,
satisfied, lazy,
unsure and careless of reality,
of a banana cut in half, or of strawberries missing
from the milky sugared cereal,
and bird wings,
the cord of the shade swaying in the breeze,
subtle, the frame of the window holds still...

The toes curled a beat, a pulse,
and languid the day, fully matured and living easy,
the promise half-fulfilled and half-empty
as the sky, blue and vague,

and living is a guess,
and the wonderment why, why is this this and those aren't these
and how now to rephrase your thesis
for the rest of the composition of the afternoon...

And lazily I stare, the ceiling is aware
of my eyes it reflects in some philosophical way,
unregistered, unacknowledged,
as I came back from the wood mill some twenty years ago
and slept with a cigarette,
with the sawdust still in my lungs,
not-thinking thinking-like
and the train rumbles across the dirt fields,
shaking the metal furnace frame, unheated and unneeded in the summer,
but now, in the winter, I pay dearly for the warmth
of an apartment, though it is still several months away,
so far away in this warm oblivion,
the air so thick it holds the ripe blackberries up
in front of my eyes
across the dirt fields, so clearly
that twenty winks bring back twenty years,
and yes, it was summer, and living was dizzy...

If there's a choice...

If there's a choice between reading about reality or seeing it
touch a thought as braille
        The volume of the world funnels in through a gap
In the window,
           the old factories in the industrial distance,
the salt of the bay air,
If there's a choice, I'd meditate on plum blossoms;
No, I wouldn't view flowers on horseback,
Nor would I eavesdrop on the crescendo of song and dance
behind the imperial door...

If there's a choice, I'd choose to be poor,
                    unnoticed,
Unrewarded, unfettered by robes of language, social mores,
No, if there was a choice, I'd not obey the rules of pickpockets
or dog-meat vendors,
        paperback writers, insurance salesmen, tavern bouncers,
I'd just amble,
    stare at the cracks of sidewalks,
And envision a dandelion shooting through, yellow and fine,
Or I will imagine
A blackberry vine in the inner city, growing o.k. without city rain,
Heaven's pennies it abstains from taking...

If I have some choice, I will have a morsel of rice
and some tea, hot or with ice,
And from beggar to king, if the choice was really mine,
I'd simply choose to be kind...

It's no longer night

The dawn will further split the sky,
a muffled jet
and the train roars through the empty morning
and the cinders of cities
electric lights
electrify and insectify my room
eleventh floor
industriously looking at Seattle
with my mind getting lighter
with a rim
of cranes at the harbor
this side
of the Pacific...

Consensual reality returns
And I split this typewritten page
dividing it into light and dark
for the Tao to enter
only to disappear
among the gulls of the morning...

Forum

O.K., I am going to take a forum now:
The oncoming future is vast!

From sweatshop shyness to unfettered Beat poetry,
From the crashing waves of the Pacific coast to a thimble of wine,
From the furniture factory to a seat at the University,
From the newspapers the homeless man is cradling to a medical prescription,
The forum for the future is vast...

More than glacier ice, more than Indonesian rice,
More than a cold night in the woods,
Things are coming out now,
And rain is beginning to fall
On princess and pauper alike,
And contradictions tightly interlock...

I am going to take this forum,
a dandelion in the inner city,
a letter from the other side of the world,
a microchip and garlic dip,
blinking lights,
a signal from a heretofore presumed dead planet,
over the dead silences of the vastness of time and space,
intelligence is coming,
we stop the moment and seize the orange in the sky
and take this forum:
the oncoming future is vast!

ABOUT KOON WOON

Koon Woon was born in a small village near Canton in 1949, immigrated to the United States in 1960, and presently resides in Seattle's International District. His poetry has appeared in numerous literary journals and anthologies, including *The Poem and the World: An International Anthology* and *Premonitions: The Kaya Anthology of New Asian North American Poetry.* Publisher of the literary 'zine, *Chrysanthemum,* and Goldfish Press, Woon is a vocal advocate for Seattle literature. *The Truth in Rented Rooms* is his first poetry collection.

206-31 7 7/6